Essentially Being Banaban In a Changing World

Law, Culture and Identity

Raobeia Ken Sigrah
Stacey M. King

BANABAN VISION PUBLICATIONS
GOLD COAST, AUSTRALIA

Essentially Being Banaban in a Changing World: Law, Culture and Identity
Copyright © Raobeia Ken Sigrah and Stacey M. King.
All rights reserved.
Published by Banaban Vision Publications
PO Box 1116 Paradise Point. Qld. 4216. Australia
www.banabanvision.com

 A catalogue record for this work is available from the National Library of Australia

ISBNs: Paperback: 978-1-7641559-0-8
Ebook: 978-1-7641559-1-5

This book may not be reproduced in any form or by any electronic or mechanical means, including information storage and retrieval system, without permission in writing from the authors. The only exception is a reviewer who may quote short excerpts in a review.

Cover designed by Stacey King

This content was adapted from a paper presented by the authors at:
ISLANDS of the WORLD VIII International Conference
"Changing Islands – Changing Worlds"
1-7 November 2004, Kinmen Island (Quemoy), Taiwan

The authors have provided information sourced from original documents, photographs, and interviews, which are either owned or kindly donated to the authors. All other reference material has been sourced as quoted. Internal diagrams were created and/or supplied by the authors.

DEDICATION

Raobeia Ken Sigrah

1956-2021
Banaban Clan spokesman and historian

Your name will live on in history as a true Banaban warrior and a proud descendant of his people, who gave your people the greatest gift:

"Hold your head high and be forever proud of being BANABAN and ensure Banaban identity is never lost but passed on to future generations".

"Te Rii ni Banaba is more than law—it is our heartbeat. Without it, we are scattered voices drifting in uncertainty; with it, we stand as one, bound by the wisdom and strength of our ancestors."

Raobeia Ken Sigrah

"The Banabans' connection to their homeland is an unbreakable bond, carried across generations —even while living far away in foreign lands."

Stacey M. King

Contents

Introduction 1
1. Abara Banaba – Our Homeland Banaba 5
2. The Banabans 7
3. The Backbone of Banaba 9
4. Culture, Customs and Traditions 11
5. *Te Inaaki* Maneaba System 15
6. Banaban Villages and Individual Land Holdings 17
7. The Colonial Village System and Its Impact 19
8. Banaban Traditional Law as Foundation of *Kabowi* (Island Court) 21
9. Fragmentation of Banaban Cultural Law Under Colonial Influence 25
10. Colonial Governance and Mining 27
11. Struggles Between Officials and the Company 29
12. World War II: The Final Blow to Banaban Sovereignty 31
13. Resettlement on Rabi, Fiji 35
14. Establishing a New Community 37
15. Financial Independence and Cultural Preservation 39
16. Banaban Financial Concerns 41
17. Banabans Living Between Two Nations 45
    Rabi, Fiji 45
    Banaba, Kiribati 47

18. Clan Spokesman: Ensuring Ethnic Survival 51
19. Balancing Tradition and Modernity 53
20. A Blended Approach: Tradition Meets Governance 55
21. Gender Equality and Cultural Tensions 57
22. Securing Banaban Rights in a Globalised World 59
23. Preserving Banaban Heritage and Cultural Identity 61
24. Honoring Banaban Identity 65
References 67
About the Authors 71
Other Titles By The Authors 77

Photographs

1. Map of Banaba with sacred Te Aka sites. 3
2. Pulang, Banaban Elder from Uma Village, Banaba. 4
3. Banaban Elder Temate, mistaken as King 1901. 6
4. *Te Tabo ni Kauti* – terrace for *te kauti* ritual. 10
5. Importance placement *maneaba* roofing. 13
6. *Te Inaaki* system, *maneaba* sitting positions. 14
7. Banaban Social Organisation. 20
8. Native Court House, Banaba 1920s. 24
9. Banaban girls wearing Mother Hubbards. 26
10. Albert Ellis at Japanese surrender Banaba 1945. 33
11. Map Rabi location in the Fiji Group. 34
12. Harry Maude, Banaba Lands Commissioner 1930s...36
13. Nei Katanoata, Banaban Dancing Group 1946. 40
14. Banaban elders during UK Court case 1970s. 43
15. Banabans moved to Rabi, Fiji. 44
16. Rabi Council of Leaders 2007. 49
17. Rabi Council of Leaders 2003. 50
18. Rabi Council of Leaders Sept 2003 50
19. Rabi Administrator with Fiji PM 2025. 52
20. Rabi Administrator looking at digitised maps. 54

21. Makin Karoro, first woman elected RCL 1996............ 56
22. Elders who signed Scandalous Document 1900. 58
23. Banaban Elders Rabi, Fiji 1997.. 60
24. Banaban MP, Tibanga Taratai and Elders 2019.......... 63
25. Authors return Te Aka ancestral remains 2000......... 64
26. Authors meet Dr Lampert ANU, Canberra 1997. 66
27. Authors with Australian Multicultural Affairs Minister Brisbane 2004. 76

Introduction

This book is being written at a time in Banaban history when profound changes and development are urgently needed—not only in a physical sense but also in mindset and outlook. If Banabans are to retain their ethnic identity over the next century, adaptation must come with education that expands perspectives, introduces new ideas, and opens pathways to opportunity and prosperity. However, change also carries risks. Without careful navigation, it could erode the cultural practices that have made the Banabans a distinct Oceanic people.

How can Banabans embrace the future while safeguarding their dreams of self-determination and cultural identity? For generations, the foundation of Banaban education rested within the family and community, passed down through revered elders. The knowledge they shared was essential for survival, shaping a disciplined society where inherited roles and responsibilities revolved around land and family heritage. This structure, known as *Te Rii Ni Banaba*—the Backbone of Banaba—guided Banaban life for centuries, enabling them to withstand invasions, famine, drought, disease, war, mining, and ultimately, the forced displacement and resettlement in Fiji. Through every hardship, their resilience was rooted in their traditions.

Today, Banabans face new challenges. Poverty makes daily survival an all-consuming struggle, and formal education under the Western system has become a highly sought-after means of securing a better future. Yet, in this pursuit of modern learning, traditional knowledge must not be overlooked. Instead, Banabans must develop programs that protect and integrate their cultural heritage into contemporary education.

As a displaced people under the governance of two Pacific nations—Fiji and Kiribati—Banabans must recognise their inherent strengths and vulnerabilities. They must allow their physically able youth to power their canoe, seeking out new opportunities, while their elders stabilise and navigate their course. Young Banabans possess keen vision, identifying new ideas that can shape a successful future. Yet, for this progress to preserve the essence of Banaban culture, it must be anchored in the wisdom, strength, and endurance passed down through generations.

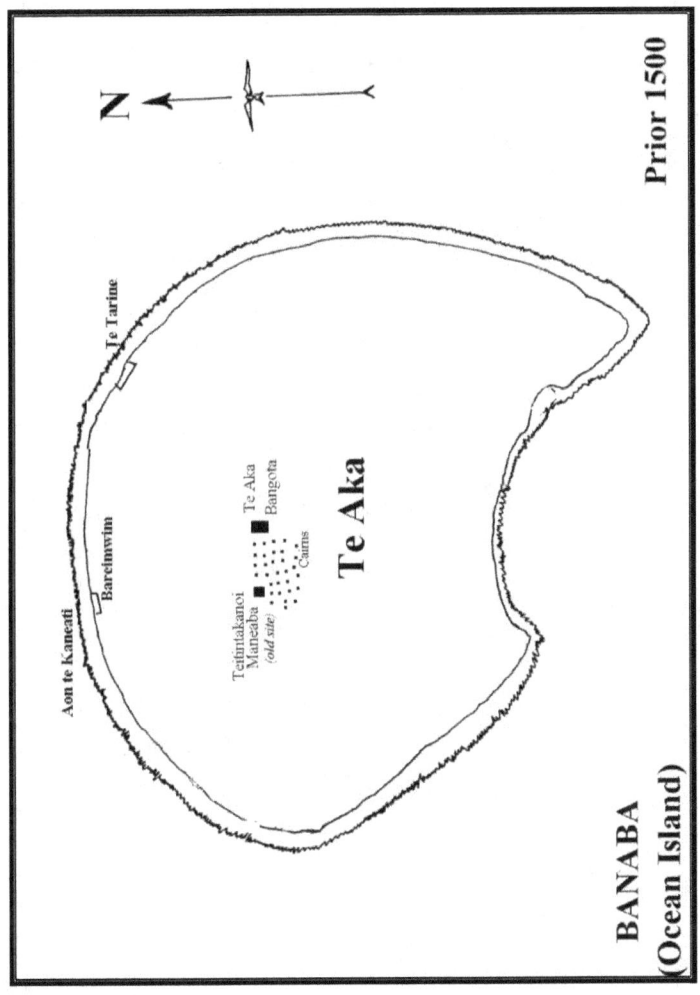

1. Map of Banaba (Ocean Island) prior to 1500 showing sacred sites of Te Aka people. Sketched by R.K. Sigrah. Digital design S.M. King.

2. Pulang, Banaban Elder from Uma Village, Banaba.
Photograph taken by Albert Ellis 1900.

1. Abara Banaba – Our Homeland Banaba

The once-lush island of Banaba, nestled near the equator at latitude 0.50° south and longitude 169.530° east, was the ancestral home of the Banabans, an isolated Oceanic people. Spanning just 595 hectares, Banaba stood alone in the vast Pacific, with its closest neighbor, Nauru, lying 180 kilometers to the southwest. Like all Indigenous Pacific Islanders, the Banabans held their land as their most treasured possession, inseparable from their identity and way of life.

The Banabans believed their ancestors were autochthones, the original creators of Banaban culture, customs, and traditions. This deep-rooted connection to their land and heritage remains intrinsic to the identity of Banaban descendants today.

However, in 1900, Albert Ellis discovered that Banaba was composed of pure phosphate rock. What followed was a devastating exploitation of the

Banabans' innocence and hospitality, culminating in the destruction of their homeland and their forced removal. This injustice, an unfathomable loss, continues to weigh heavily on the hearts and minds of every Banaban.

3. Banaban Elder Temate,(front row-second from right) mistaken by Albert Ellis as King of Banaba. Photograph taken by Albert Ellis 1901 Tabwewa Village.

2. The Banabans

The origins of the Banaban people were preserved through oral history, passed down through storytelling, myths, legends, singing, chanting, and dance—traditions that connected each generation to their ancestors. This enduring legacy formed the foundation of Banaban identity, shaping their understanding of lineage, governance, and cultural unity.

Archaeological research conducted by R.J. Lampert at Te Aka village in 1964 provided critical evidence of Banaba's indigenous population. His findings supported the Banaban claim that their ancestry was distinct from Polynesian lineage—a conclusion further reinforced through forensic examination of skeletal remains (Lampert 1968:18; Sigrah & King 2001:35). Prior to Lampert's discovery, Pacific historians and archaeologists theorised that the *"old Banabans,"* regarded by Banabans as a people of pure lineage, were actually a mixture of two distinct groups: the *"long-jawed and short-jawed people"* (Lampert 1965:3). Early scholars described them as *"small-bodied, squat, crinkly-haired, large-eared, and black-skinned"* (H.E. Maude 1932), suggesting a Melanesian origin (Grace 1964; Bellwood 1979; Irwin 1992; Grimble MS n.d., cited in Maude & Maude 1994:105; Sigrah & King 2001:27).

The first major outside contact for the Banabans came in the 1500s, with the invasion of the Auriaria clan from Gilolo in the East Indies (Sigrah & King 2001:91). Before this encounter, the Te Aka people lived in relative isolation, holding a deeply rooted belief that Banaba was the centre of the world. According to oral tradition, they viewed themselves with a profound sense of freedom and self-sufficiency, embracing their identity with unwavering pride:

"With discrete knowledge and self-contentment, the Te Aka clan regarded Banaba as the centre of the world. They held feelings of freedom and superiority at the very core of their awareness, forming the nucleus of being Te Aka, the indigenous people of Banaba." (Sigrah & King 2001)

This deep cultural consciousness formed the backbone of Banaban society, shaping their resilience in the face of external influences and historical upheavals.

3. The Backbone of Banaba

Te rii ni Banaba forms the foundation of Banaban traditional law, serving as a guideline for resolving disputes over land ownership, lineage, inherited cultural roles, and broader moral issues within families, clans, and the community. This ancient framework is at the core of Banaban ethnic identity, built upon three fundamental principles:

Katea rikim! — Recite your genealogy!
Tera taum? — What is your family's inherited role?
Arana am Kainga! — Name your land!

The Banabans believe that earning respect in society requires a deep understanding of tradition and culture. To achieve this, one must know their family's genealogy, recognise their inherited role and duty from birth, and understand their place within the intricate structure of the Banaban clan system (Sigrah & King 2001:56). These three interwoven pillars of knowledge form the essence of

Banaban identity—an identity inseparably linked to their land.

Before the arrival of Europeans, Banaban society was highly disciplined and structured. While the island was divided into distinct districts representing family *kainga* (hamlets) and clans, the Banabans lived harmoniously as one people. Today, with most Banabans residing on Rabi Island in Fiji, the principles of traditional law embodied in *te rii ni Banaba* continue to be upheld, remaining deeply rooted in the customs and ancestral land of Banaba.

4. *Te Tabo ni Kauti* - private terrace for *te kauti* ritual (Williams 1901–1931).

4. Culture, Customs and Traditions

Banabans trace the roots of their culture to the ancient *Te Aka* belief system, which centered on sun and ancestral worship. This spiritual framework involved sacred relics—such as ancestral skulls—and rituals invoking spirits through sorcery. These beliefs were protected by strict protocols, classified as "taboo" and sacred. In Banaban philosophy, breaking these rules could invoke a curse, reinforcing a deep culture of respect and caution. Over time, this fear strengthened the custom of reverence, entwining respect with the mystery and power of the *Te Aka*, known for their exceptional sorcery skills.

The discovery of phosphate on Banaba marked the beginning of widespread misinterpretation of Banaban history. One example is Maude (1932), whose accounts incorrectly linked significant aspects of Banaban social organisation, particularly sun worship and ceremonial rituals, to the wrong clans and hamlets. His references to "the black folks" should have described the *Te Aka* clan, yet he misidentified them as the *Mangati* clan. Furthermore, Maude mistook the *Te Aka* people for the inhabitants of *Tairua*, a name that does not denote a specific place or people in Banaban history. Instead, *Tairua* is recognised as the name of a battle fought between the indigenous *Te Aka* and the invading *Auriaria* clan—the word itself meaning "foreigner" (Sigrah & King 2001:92).

Colonial officials such as Maude and Grimble frequently sent reports to the British Colonial Office in London during their oversight of phosphate mining. Their interpretations, shaped by colonial perspectives, later became recognised as historical records, aligning Banaban identity with I-Kiribati culture rather than preserving its distinct heritage. The Banabans argue that these accounts were written more for colonial propaganda than genuine historical reconstruction.

Another notable misrepresentation occurred during Albert Ellis' early mining negotiations, when he mistakenly assumed he was dealing with a Banaban chief. Although Ellis later corrected his error, subsequent historians—including Grimble and Maude—continued to perpetuate the false notion of a Banaban chiefly system. This interpretation was based on European models of governance, which did not reflect Banaban society. Traditional Banaban leadership was rooted in a patriarchal clan system governed by elders under the protocols of *Te Rii Ni Banaba*.

5. The importance of the placement of roofing in maneaba structures (Williams Collection 1905-31).

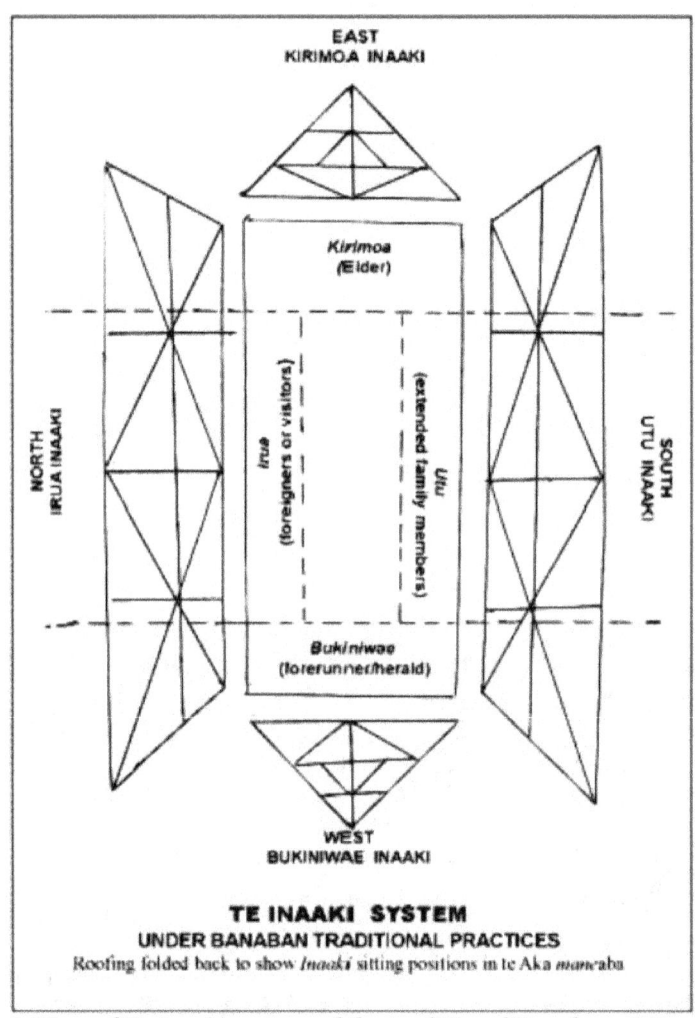

6. View of *Te Inaaki* system of the traditional Banaban sitting positions within Te Aka *maneaba*. Original sketch Raobeia Ken Sigrah and digital design Stacey M. King.

5. *Te Inaaki* Maneaba System

Banaban society followed a structured order known as *Te Inaaki*—translated as "a tier of thatch on a roof" (Bingham 1908:16). This system reflected the hierarchy of Banaban governance and dictated seating arrangements within the village *maneaba* (meeting house). Clan elders sat on the eastern side, signifying the power of the rising sun, while the *bukiniwae* (herald) sat on the western side, representing sunset and the close of day. Other clan members occupied the southern side, while the northern side was reserved for *irua* (visitors). The east-to-west placement symbolised the sacred connection the *Te Aka* people held with their sun totem.

The sun was not only a source of spiritual power but also a guide for timekeeping and ceremonial protocols. Meetings would begin in the morning with the elders speaking first and conclude at the end of the day, when the *bukiniwae* would depart to spread news across villages and hamlets.

In other Banaban settlements, different *maneaba* protocols reflected distinct ancestral traditions. Communities in Tabwewa, Uma, and Tabiang followed *Te Boti*, a system defining one's rightful place within the *maneaba* structure. Unlike *Te Inaaki*, *Te Boti* was recorded in historical accounts and later confused with Kiribati practices, leading to misinterpretations of Banaban customs (Maude & Maude 1995:43; Grimble 1989:115-129). These differing *maneaba* systems reveal how social organisation, traditional law, and leadership were deeply embedded in Banaban heritage.

The Banaban term *Batua* (pronounced *Pat-u-are*) is an ancient word signifying a godfather, deity, or ancestral figurehead—an enduring testament to the spiritual and hierarchical foundations of Banaban society.

6. Banaban Villages and Individual Land Holdings

The Banabans had no prior understanding of the village system, and elders argue that, at that point in their history, no formal village structure was in place (Sigrah & King, 2001:218). The concept of a "village" was only introduced in the 1800s when English and American whalers, stopping to collect fresh provisions, referred to Banaban settlements as villages (Sigrah & King, 2001:177). By the time ethnographer Arthur Mahaffy recorded Banaban life in 1900, he identified four villages: Uma, Tabiang, Tabwewa, and Buakonikai.

However, historically, Banaba was originally divided into five districts, each corresponding with significant events in Banaban history. The first invasion, led by Auriaria and his party in the 1500s, established the Tabwewa district, while the arrival of Nei Anginimaeao in the 1600s resulted in the formation of Tabiang. Before their arrival, the island's original inhabitants resided in an area called te Aonnoanne—meaning "that place!"—which contained te Aka ("the first hamlet") and was home to those later referred to as *te moa ni kainga*. Other districts emerged as new arrivals settled: Toakira, allocated to Nei Teborata and her followers, and Uma, given to Na Maninimate, a member of Nei Anginimaeao's party. Despite its name meaning "lagoon side of the island," Banaba has no true lagoon; instead, Uma refers to the most sheltered region of the island's shoreline (Sigrah & King, 2001:125).

Before European influence reshaped Banaban settlements, each district contained key structures:
- Numerous individual *mwenga* (houses)
- Several *kainga* (hamlets)
- One *maneaba* (district meeting house)
- One *uma n anti* (spirit house)
- Multiple *uma n teinako* (houses for menstruating women)
- One *uma n roronga* (young men's house, near district terraces)
- Several *bareaka* (canoe sheds)
- Terraces for practicing *te kauti* (sorcery)
- A playground for district games
- *Bangabanga* (water caves) owned by specific clans (Sigrah & King, 2001:220).

7. The Colonial Village System and Its Impact

The introduction of the European-style village system marked one of the most profound disruptions in Banaban society. Banabans believe this system was implemented by the colonial government at the request of the mining company to facilitate land acquisitions and leases.

By centralising the population into villages, authorities could exert greater control over Banaban land use, clearing the way for phosphate extraction.

This shift fractured Banaban heritage and social structures. The forced relocation of families from their traditional hamlets led to the dissolution of clan-based socialisation.

A striking example of this upheaval is the amalgamation of the original *te Aka* and *Toakira* clan hamlets into Buakonikai village. In the process, the *Toakira* clan, less dominant than *te Aka*, lost its heritage, while much of its land was absorbed by the mining industry (Sigrah & King, 2001:216, 226–229).

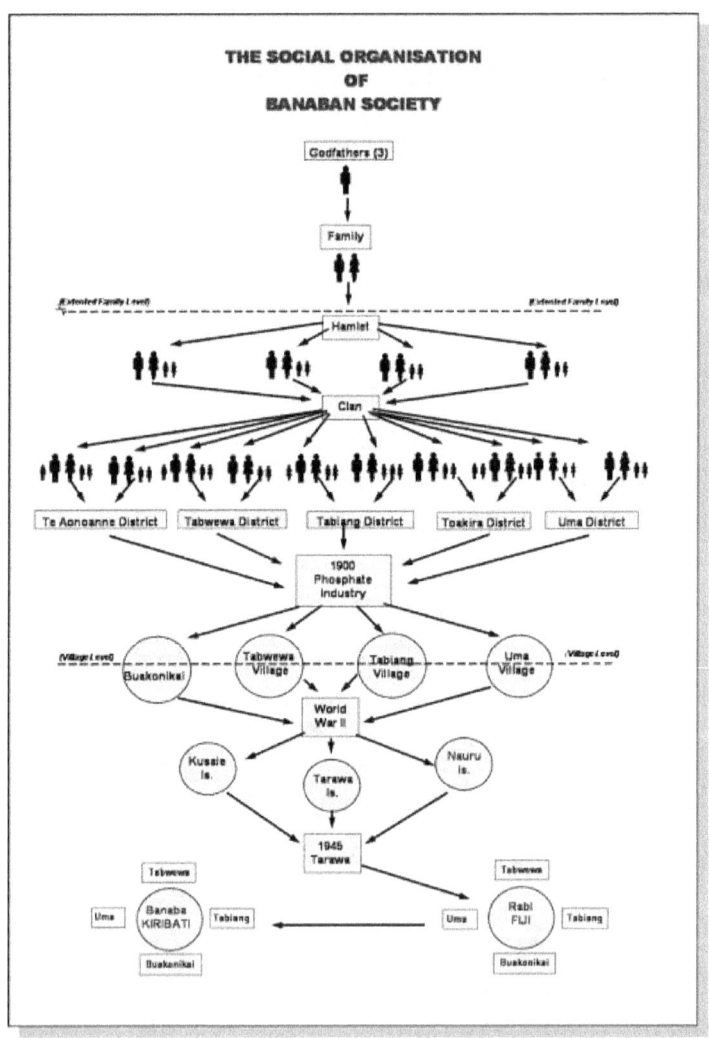

7. Banaban Social Organisation. Original by Raobeia Ken Sigrah and digital design Stacey M. King.

8. Banaban Traditional Law as Foundation of *Kabowi* (Island Court)

During colonial rule on Banaba, an Island Court was established based on British law. However, the Banabans remained deeply committed to their traditional legal system and were reluctant to accept the newly imposed foreign regulations. This created a challenge for the colonial government, which sought to avoid unrest while negotiating land acquisitions with Banaban landowners on behalf of the British Phosphate Commission (BPC). In response, the court system was modified to incorporate Banaban customary law as its foundation for local governance, though it remained under the authority of a European magistrate.

Unbeknownst to the Banabans, this system—built upon their own respect for traditional law—would ultimately be used against them. Arthur

Grimble, in *A Pattern of Islands*, reflects on this dynamic:

> The effect of the truly remarkable initiative wielded by the native courts and the representative's nature of their constitution was to keep alive among them (quite independently of European supervision) a high sense of responsibility for their decisions and maintain among the people at large a vivid and critical interest on the conduct of their own affairs. The *Kabowi* system was established by an extraordinarily wise dispensation of the eighteen nineties. 'Wise' is not to imply that the panel code was entirely devoid of flaws; for example, it forced monogamy, under pain of imprisonment, upon a historically polygynous people and made criminal offences of certain sex-relationships that were basic to the old moralities. That was itself a moral and anthropological crime of first magnitude, which no British missionary body or government would have dared to attempt, even in those days, against a more powerful community. But for all that, the *Kabowi* system as a whole stood for an almost unique effort, in the heyday of Imperialism and thirty years before the publication of Lord Lugard's Dual

Mandate, to engage the genius of a subject race on a really big scale in vital business of self-rule' (Grimble 1952:97).

Grimble's observations highlight both the paradox and the consequences of the colonial court system. While it allowed Banabans a degree of self-governance, it was also a tool of control—one that shaped their legal and social structures in ways they did not initially foresee:

> ...when the law by means of its necessary agent, force, imposes upon men a regulation of labor, a method or a subject or education, a religious faith or creed – then the law is no longer negative; it acts positively upon people. It substitutes the will of the legislator for their own wills; the initiative of the legislator for their own initiatives. When this happens, the people no longer need to discuss, to compare, to plan ahead; 'it being intended that' the law does all this for them. Intelligence becomes a useless prop for the people; they cease to be men; they lose their personality, their liberty, their property. (Frederic Bastiat 1850).

8. Native Court House, Banaba (BPC Archives circa 1920s).

9. Fragmentation of Banaban Cultural Law Under Colonial Influence

The arrival of traders and the introduction of Christianity were the first footholds of Western influence that began to reshape Banaban society. Foreign traders enticed Banabans with much-sought-after items such as knives, cheap ornaments, and glass, often bartering for prised shark teeth swords and shark fins. Meanwhile, missionaries imposed fines on wayward congregants, requiring payment in coconuts. By the time phosphate mining operations began, a significant portion of Banaban wealth—over one-third of their modest incomes—was flowing into mission coffers (Binder, 1977:26; Sigrah & King, 2001:198).

During this era, books, especially Bibles, became highly valued possessions, alongside Western-style clothing meant to cover "heathen nakedness." With the arrival of the mining company, more than half of the Banaban population had converted to Christianity, embracing the belief that they were sinners in the eyes of God and that the word of the white man carried divine authority, as proclaimed by King George V. Under this totalitarian influence, missionaries instructed Banabans to abandon their ancestral customs.

However, not all Banabans were willing to relinquish their traditions, destroy their coral deities, forsake their sacred frigate birds, or become laborers to afford modest missionary attire such as *Mother Hubbard dresses and cotton trousers* (Binder, 1977:26). Those who resisted—led by their elders—became known as *tani Bekan* (Pagans) and stood firm in upholding their old ways.

9. Banaban girls wearing Mother Hubbard's (Williams Collection 1901-31).

10. Colonial Governance and Mining

Up until 1908, the mining company dictated most of the local rules on Banaba, despite the unclear legal framework surrounding its land acquisitions. Early on, Ellis secured large portions of Banaban land before the British formally raised their flag, believing the transactions would be legitimised under future British law.

Meanwhile, colonial officials took the stance that Banaba had automatically become a British possession the moment the company was granted a mining license—regardless of when the flag-raising actually occurred. In reality, phosphate extraction began under dubious legal circumstances, with no clear blueprint for Banaba's future (Williams & Macdonald, 1985:88).

By 1909, Banaba was designated as the headquarters for the Resident Commissioner of the Gilbert and Ellice Islands Colony. The Resident

Com-missioner, Telfer Campbell, had spent twelve years in spartan isolation in the Gilberts before being abruptly transferred to Banaba, where he was provided with comparatively luxurious amenities. However, Campbell soon found himself engulfed by the phosphate industry's interests. He maintained a long-standing conflict with missionaries, resenting their influence over the local population, yet was swiftly reassigned to Tonga.

His temporary replacement, Acting Resident Commissioner Mahaffy—who had first visited Banaba in 1896, was deeply disturbed by the island's industrialised state and the company's treatment of the Banabans. He urged the Colonial Office in Fiji to compel the mining company to adopt a land rehabilitation program. However, his pleas fell on deaf ears, and he soon realised the extent of the company's power—even within British government circles in London. Mahaffy warned that if the company continued unchecked in its mining operations, Banaba would eventually become uninhabitable.

11. Struggles Between Officials and the Company

Mahaffy's successor, Captain John Quayle Dickson R.N., arrived from Africa with a clear mandate: *"to satisfy within legal parameters the needs of both the Banabans and the Phosphate Company"* (Williams & Macdonald, 1985:89). However, upon witnessing the island's deteriorating state, he quickly recognised the difficulty of his position.

Dickson proposed that Banabans contribute to a Trust Fund that would allow them to purchase a new island in the future. The company, however, argued that relocating the Banabans would be too costly. He also voiced concerns about the company's mining methods, which were destroying food-bearing trees and eroding Banaban livelihoods. In response, Dickson refused to register any more "Phosphate and Trees" leases until the company adopted a more systematic approach, ensuring mining sites were worked to their limits before expanding operations and minimising the destruction of crucial resources. He further insisted the company should pay more for the land it acquired.

Despite sporadic interventions by colonial officials, each successive government representative who sought to curb the company's exploitation ultimately failed, falling victim to its overwhelming influence. Leading up to World War II, officials recognised the devastating effects of mining, yet the colonial administration remained largely paralysed, reluctant to disrupt phosphate production.

By 1921, the privately owned British mining company was acquired by a joint consortium representing three governments: the United Kingdom, Australia, and New Sealand. From that point forward, Banabans unknowingly found themselves facing even more formidable adversaries.

While these political struggles played out behind the scenes, Banabans remained focused on the immediate reality before them—the irreversible destruction of their homeland. Even as they fought to preserve their customs, culture, and traditions, the land itself was slipping away. For them, the situation was clear: *"When the land goes and our sacred waterholes go... we too, seem to be lost!"* (Sigrah, 1998).

12. World War II: The Final Blow to Banaban Sovereignty

The Japanese invasion of Banaba in 1942 marked a turning point that ultimately sealed the fate of Banaban hopes for defending their homeland against relentless phosphate mining. Before World War II, Japan had been one of the largest buyers of Banaban phosphate outside the Commission countries.

In 1943, the Japanese occupation force forcibly removed the Banabans from their island, dispersing them to military labor camps across the Pacific—Nauru, Tarawa in the Gilbert Islands, and Kosrae in Micronesia. A few were left behind on Banaba to fish for Japanese troops. The disruption was so severe that the Banaban people feared they would never see their homeland again.

This fear became a reality when, at the war's end, the Colonial Government relocated the Banabans to Rabi Island in Fiji. Officials claimed that the

Japanese had destroyed their homes and that their villages *"no longer existed"* (Sigrah & King, 2001:258). In truth, this narrative served as propaganda, exploiting the devastation of war to justify the permanent removal of the Banabans. It was a convenient solution for both the Colonial Office and the mining company, allowing them to eliminate Banaban opposition to phosphate extraction.

As Ellis bluntly stated:

> "...until the phosphate operation was well underway again there would be no money for such social and cultural luxuries as a great communal rehabilitation scheme." (Williams & Macdonald, 1985:341; Sigrah & King, 2001:259)

Banaban resettlement was no longer framed as a matter of survival but rather dismissed as a "social and cultural luxury," secondary to the urgent priority of restoring mining operations. Banabans were now regarded as the *"Banaban problem"*—a label that signified their displacement was not just an aftermath of war but a deliberate strategy (King, 1998).

Only eleven days after the war officially ended, 100 imported laborers from the Gilbert and Ellice Islands arrived on Banaba, and mining operations resumed. By then, the Banabans—now absent from their homeland—had lost the ability to resist the political and environmental destruction unfolding on their island.

10. Albert Ellis talking to Brig. Stevenson, Australian Army at the Japanese surrender Banaba, 1 Oct 1945 (Australian War Museum).

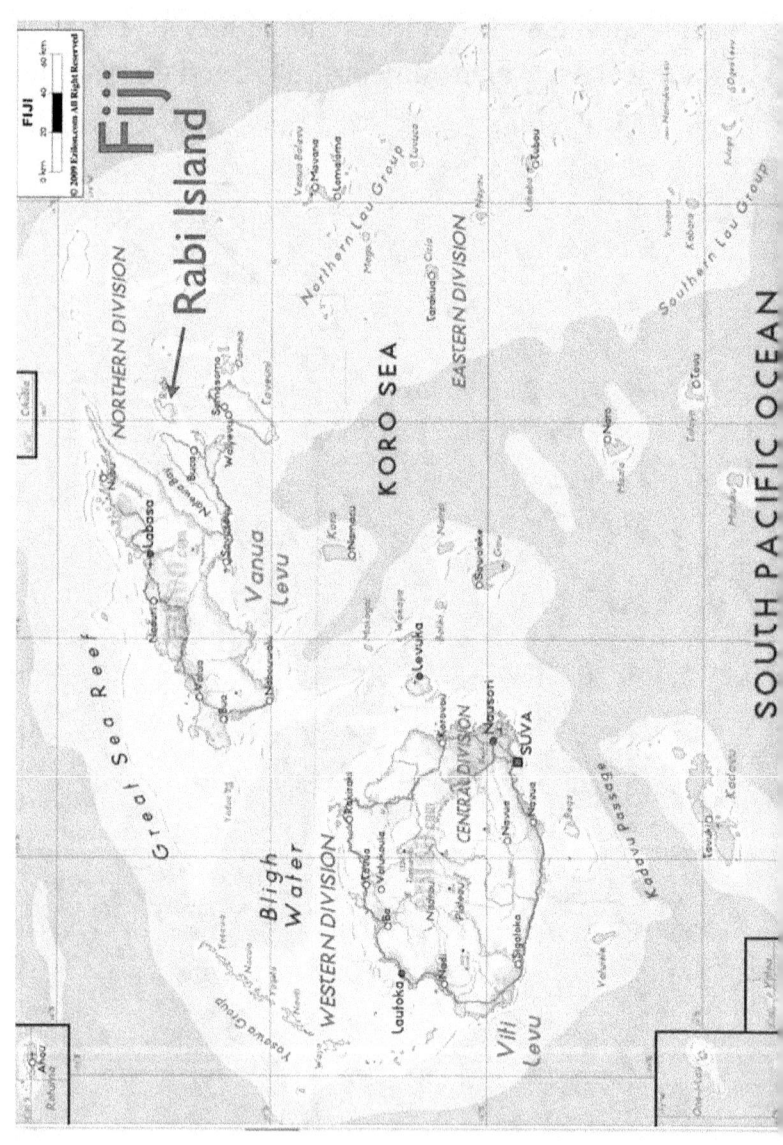

11. Map Rabi location in the Fiji Group
(https://www.banaban.com/rabi-location-fiji).

13. Resettlement on Rabi, Fiji

On 15 December 1945, the Banabans arrived on Rabi Island in Fiji. By this point, they were convinced that King George V and the British Empire had betrayed them twice—first by annexing Banaba into the Gilbert and Ellice Islands Colony, and then by relocating the surviving population of 703 Banabans and 300 I-Kiribati, a total of 1,003 people, 3,200 kilometers away from their homeland. Until then, the Banabans had never even heard of Rabi, a place far removed from the land of their ancestors.

The conditions awaiting them were a stark contrast to what British officials had promised. Accommodation consisted of hastily erected army tents, which provided little protection against the relentless tropical downpours of Fiji's cyclone season (Sigrah & King, 2001:260). The two-month supply of army rations soon proved insufficient, and the Banabans struggled to adapt to their unfamiliar surroundings.

By 1946, Henry Maude, Chief Land Commissioner for the Gilbert and Ellice Islands Colony, expressed concerns about the Banabans' future, both in terms of their land and finances:

"...fifteen years ago, I spent nearly a year working among them in their villages (when I got to know intimately a generation now almost extinct), and since then contact has been renewed periodically until the war. It seems to me that the community has progressively degenerated morally and physically, and that urgent measures are now indicated if they are not to sink into a state of indolence or apathy" (Maude, 1946:17).

12. Harry Maude, Chief Lands Commissioner Banaba 1930s.

14. Establishing a New Community

As the realities of their situation set in, Banaban elders took charge, uniting the people in an effort to rebuild their community. They organised settlements into four villages named after their original homes on Banaba—Buakonikai, Tabwewa, Uma, and Tabiang. Each village was settled based on traditional land rights inherited from Banaba.

To preserve Banaban identity and cultural traditions, elders conducted general meetings based on customary practices. These gatherings ensured that vital rites and ceremonies—integral to Banaban heritage—were revived and maintained despite their displacement.

From the 1960s to 1979, the Banabans began exercising a degree of self-governance. Royalty payments from phosphate mining on Banaba provided them with the resources to implement community programs and local initiatives. Their governance structure was formalised through the Banaban Settlement Ordinance of 1945, which established the Rabi Island Council. The first general elections on Rabi were held in 1957 and continued every three years. Banabans became subject to Fijian taxation and entitled to government services. The Banaban Settlement Ordinance also created the Rabi Island Fund, designed to manage finances with specified powers and restrictions. Over the years, additional legislation followed:

- **Banaban Funds Ordinance (Cap. 105)** – Establishing the Banaban Trust Fund Board
- **Banaban Land Ordinance (Cap. 117)** – Enacted in 1965
- **Banaban Settlement Act (1970)** – Replacing previous ordinances, formally recognising the role of the Banaban Adviser, and appointing the Rabi Island Court under a Magistrate designated by the Governor

15. Financial Independence and Cultural Preservation

During this period, while royalty funds were available, Banabans allocated significant resources toward preserving their customs—traditional dances, games, wedding ceremonies, and other cultural practices brought from Banaba. They also embarked on extensive building projects on Rabi and sent their children to mainland Fiji for education.

Managing finances was a new challenge for the Banabans, who lacked formal financial training or external assistance. They were tasked not only with administrating Rabi's local governance but also with supporting Banabans who had chosen to return to Banaba. Additionally, they were responsible for overseeing mining royalties held in trust by the Banaban Trust Fund Board on behalf of individual landowners with leases on Banaba.

Despite their displacement, the Banabans remained determined to sustain their traditions and self-sufficiency, striving to preserve their identity while navigating the complexities of their new existence in Fiji.

13. Banaban Dancing Group called Nei Katanoata, upholding Banaban culture on Rabi (Frank Christopher 1946).

16. Banaban Financial Concerns

By 1965, the Banabans had grown increasingly frustrated with decades of disputes over their land leases on Banaba and the inadequate royalties they were receiving. They had come to the painful realisation that the British Government had no genuine interest in safeguarding their affairs. With trust in the government lost, they took the final step of instigating legal proceedings in the British courts (Sigrah & King, 2001:18).

In 1979, the courts ruled that the British Government had been guilty of *moral negligence*, compelling both the British Government and the British Phosphate Commission to negotiate a settlement. It took four years for the Banabans to finally accept the offered compensation of A$10 million, which was placed in trust. Fiji's legislation was subsequently amended to facilitate the creation and disbursement of the Banaban Trust Fund.

However, while the payout stipulated that only the income generated from the fund could be withdrawn, a *Rabi Council Affairs* report from 1994 revealed significant legal uncertainties:

> "There was no Trust Deed or, so far as we can trace, any legally registered letter or agreement."

The report also raised concerns regarding governmental control over the fund's administration:

> "The establishment of the Fund and its administration, along with the capital preservation requirement, were embodied—by amendment in 1981—in the Banaban Settlement Act... and may be subject to constitutional constraints or amended by the Fiji Legislature without reference to or assent of the donors."

Ironically, the Banabans viewed the A$10 million as an inadequate compensation for generations of exploitation, yet at an international level, the fund was classified as a *development fund.* As a result, Banabans, already marginalised as a minority community, were largely excluded from mainstream development programs.

A 2002 United Nations International Human Rights report (Section 38) acknowledged the severe social impact of this exclusion:

> "Since the 1980s, all indicators for the social well-being of the community have shown a serious decline."

The forced removal of the Banabans from their homeland and their subsequent resettlement on Rabi left an indelible mark on the community's legacy of displacement, financial instability, and systemic neglect that continues to shape their reality today.

14. Banaban elders in London during UK Court case (British Newspaper photo) 1970s.

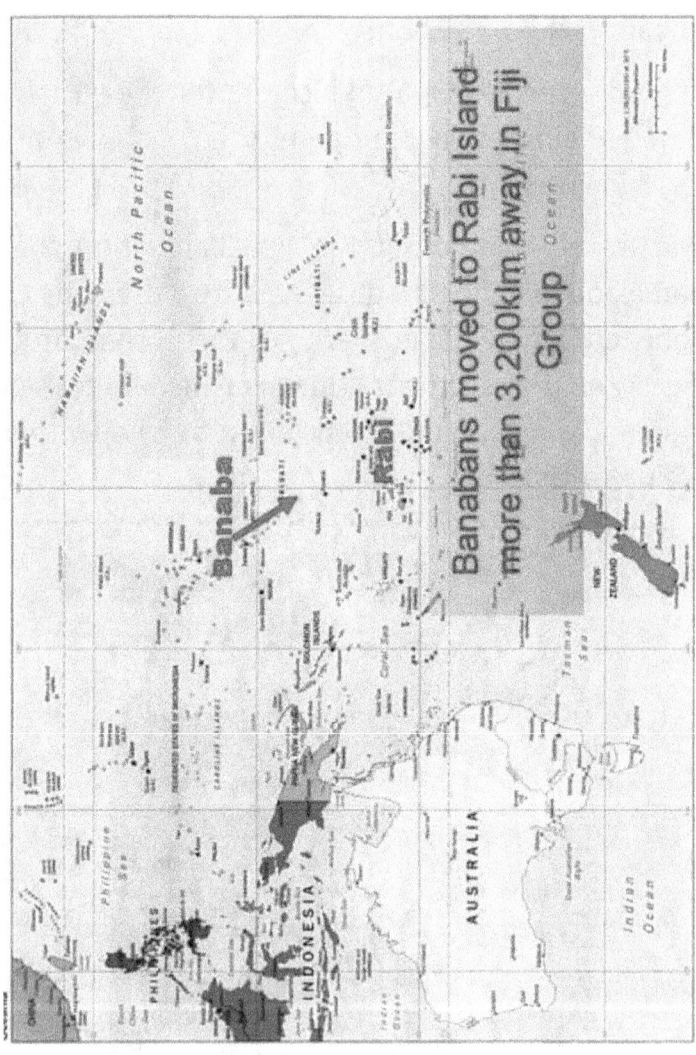

15. Banabans from Banaba (Ocean Island), Kiribati moved to Rabi, Fiji. Today they are under the governance of two nations (Banaban Vision Archive).

17. Banabans Living Between Two Nations

Rabi, Fiji

Today, Banabans living in Fiji face complex cultural challenges. Unlike the Fijian system, which places paramount importance on chieftainship, Banaban tradition does not recognise chiefs as part of social organisation. This cultural distinction presents a dilemma for Banabans, who remain deeply aware of their status as guests on indigenous freehold land.

The question of their long-term acceptance in Fiji has become particularly pressing in light of the political instability caused by the 1987 and 2000 coups. These events, aimed at reinforcing ethnic Fijian political dominance, heightened concerns about the security of Banaban land tenure on Rabi. Comparisons have even been drawn to land resumption policies in Zimbabwe, another former Commonwealth nation.

Even today, Banabans are expected to pay tribute to the *Tui Cakau*, the Paramount Chief of Cakaudrove District, by providing food, mats, and other gifts for chiefly ceremonies. Failure to comply with these protocols could create tensions, as Rabi falls under Cakaudrove's jurisdiction. Out of respect for Fijian traditions, Banabans continue to observe these customs, just as the island's original indigenous inhabitants did for centuries.

However, since the 1987 coup, fishing grounds around Rabi have been closed, restricting Banaban access to commercial fishing. This has made earning money for basic necessities and education increasingly difficult. Despite their willingness to adopt Fijian customs, the Banabans still struggle with their precarious status—after more than fifty years, many still feel like "guests" on Fijian soil.

Another major concern is the gradual assimilation of Banabans into mainstream Fijian culture. Whether through intermarriage or the inclusion of Fijian traditions in school curricula, the erosion of distinct Banaban identity remains a persistent worry.

Now, as more first- and second-generation Banabans born on Rabi complete their education within the Fiji system, they increasingly find themselves integrated into Fiji's government structure. With few economic opportunities on Rabi itself, their skills remain underutilised within their own community. This creates a difficult paradox: while education is vital for improving future prospects, it also accelerates the alienation of some of the most talented members of the Banaban people. Recognising this growing issue, Banaban leaders stress the urgent need to develop programs that will preserve their heritage and provide pathways for reinvestment in their own society.

Banaba, Kiribati

Banaba now falls under Kiribati's legal jurisdiction, enshrined in *Chapter IX* of the *Kiribati Constitution*. Although the majority of Banabans live in Fiji, key legal provisions protect their land rights on Banaba, including:
- Residency in Rabi does not affect a Banaban's land rights in Banaba.
- All land acquired by the Crown before Kiribati's Independence Day must be returned to Banaban landowners or their heirs once phosphate extraction is completed.
- No Banaban land may be compulsorily acquired, except for leasehold interests in accordance with Section 8(1) of the Constitution.
  - Every Banaban has an inalienable right to enter and reside in Banaba.

- Banaba shall have an Island Council, with powers and duties prescribed by law.

A significant concession within the *Kiribati Constitution* is the inclusion of two nominated Banaban representatives in the *Maneaba Ni Maungatabu* (Kiribati's House of Assembly)—one representing Banaba and the other representing Rabi.

The Rabi Council of Leaders (RCL), based in Fiji, administers Banaba at a cost of approximately F$12,000 per month (Sigrah & King, 2001). While the Kiribati government provides basic services—including postal operations, radio communication, healthcare, education, and law enforcement—the remainder is managed by the RCL through a designated Banaban Island representative.

Since phosphate mining ceased in 1979, the Kiribati government has commissioned at least two feasibility studies to explore the possibility of resuming mining operations (Roche Bros, 1987). However, economic viability concerns and opposition from Banaban landowners—most of whom now reside on Rabi—have prevented further development.

As in Fiji, Banabans seeking higher education through Kiribati scholarship programs must commit to a mandatory service period of approximately five years, effectively bonding them to the Kiribati system.

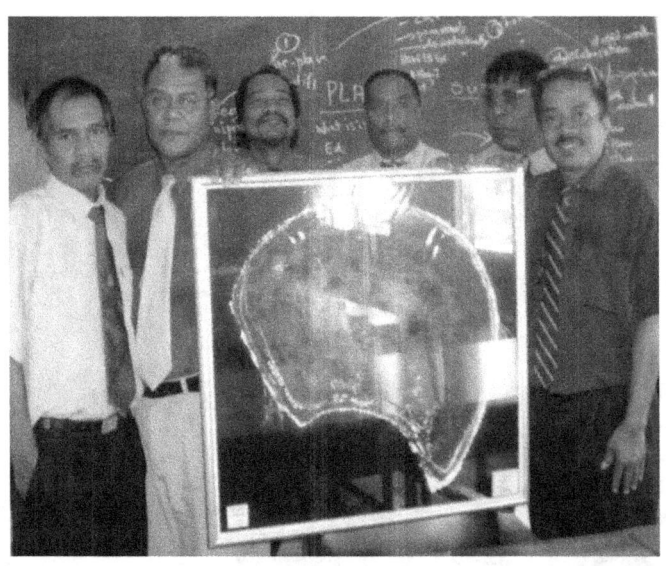

16. Rabi Council of Leaders 2007 (S.M. King Collection).

17. Rabi Council of Leaders 2003. Chairman Iakoba Karutake (3rd right). He is now the Fiji government appointed Rabi Administrator for a 3-year term January 2023 (S.M. King Collection).

18. Rabi Council of Leaders Sept 2003 (S.M. King Collection).

18. Clan Spokesman: Ensuring Ethnic Survival

In Banaban tradition, the clan spokesman has long been regarded as the representative of the elders, responsible for chairing family meetings and participating in general village discussions. From an early age, a clan spokesman receives specialised training to prepare for this role, which remains strictly non-political and focused solely on cultural matters. His duties include upholding ancestral protocols related to land ownership on Banaba, maintaining inherited roles and responsibilities, and overseeing ritual practices.

Holding this position requires deep knowledge of clan genealogies and fluency in *te rii ni Banaba* (Banaban cultural law). The role is treated with great respect and, by custom, is traditionally reserved for males. The spokesman must be related by blood to the clans he represents and is chosen by elders to speak on their behalf at official functions.

19. Rabi Administrator, Iakoba Karutake with the Hon. Prime Minister, Sitiveni Rabuka, Suva, Fiji (Fiji Times March 2025).

19. Balancing Tradition and Modernity

Between 1987 and 1989, the Banaban Council of Elders on Rabi, along with representatives from all Banaban clans, held meetings to confirm genealogies and inherited rights within the Tabwewa district. Clan-based land disputes were also resolved through these gatherings, preventing many conflicts from escalating into legal cases.

However, the influence of Western education has begun reshaping Banaban society. Younger generations are increasingly questioning elders' decisions—topics once considered taboo under traditional custom. Education has shifted Banaban lifestyles, distancing many from the customs and traditions that were once an integral part of daily life. Rather than learning directly from their elders, many now rely on books written by outside scholars to understand their own heritage.

This shift has created an *education gap* within the community. On one hand, Banabans look to their educated members for leadership, expertise in governance, finance, and development, and the ability to navigate complex Western systems. Yet, these ideals often clash with the realities of traditional society, where many Banabans still struggle to engage with Western administrative models. Bridging this gap remains a pressing challenge.

20. Iakoba Karutake, Rabi Administrator, reviewing the digitisation of maps of Banaba and Rabi land holdings, 15 Aug 2024(Rabi Council of Leaders Facebook group).

20. A Blended Approach: Tradition Meets Governance

One example of successfully integrating traditional and Western education can be seen in Fiji's system, where the Great Council of Chiefs and Fiji's Parliament merged customary practices with constitutional law. A similar approach was tested on Rabi in 1991, when the Fiji Government appointed Interim Administrators to oversee Banaban affairs. This appointment followed the Banabans' rejection of the Rabi Council of Leaders, triggering a major dispute within the community.

Over the next five years, the Interim Administrators—non-Banaban government officials—worked alongside Rabi Elders to govern the community. This cooperative model demonstrated that governance could function effectively by combining skilled professionals with the guidance and wisdom of Banaban elders.

21. Makin Karoro the first woman elected to Rabi Council of Leader 1996 (Fiji Times).

21. Gender Equality and Cultural Tensions

The 1996 Rabi Council elections brought new challenges when a woman was elected to Council for the first time. Banaban Elders argued that, under custom, these roles had always been reserved for men. Additional concerns were raised about the need to formally define the terms *Elder* and *indigenous Banaban* within their society.

When the female Councillor refused to step aside, Elders then asked to take their case to the Fiji Government. This did not eventuate when it was pointed out that under the Banaban Settlement Act, Section 3 (7), that the phrase, "*Any qualified elector may...*" was incorporated into the Act, while the word **male** was not.

With growing international pressure on Fiji's human rights policies, Banabans were ultimately required to comply with global standards for gender equality, marking a significant shift in their traditional governance system.

22. Elders who signed the Scandalous Document with Albert Ellis in 1900 (BPC Archives).

22. Securing Banaban Rights in a Globalised World

As globalisation accelerates and efforts to promote and protect human rights in the Pacific gain momentum, the recognition of cultural diversity, indigenous rights, and the importance of cultural context are more crucial than ever. For the Banabans, fundamental human rights commonly upheld in democratic societies have historically failed to protect or empower them.

In today's changing environment, Banabans must harness international laws and protocols, with the support of NGOs and global organisations, to demand the rights to which they are inherently entitled. These include:

- Economic, social, and cultural rights
- Access to essential services
- Food security and shelter
- Sustainable livelihoods

- Environmental rehabilitation and the preservation of Banaba

23. Banaban Elders Rabi, Fiji 1997 (S.M. King Collection).

23. Preserving Banaban Heritage and Cultural Identity

Banaban traditions must be safeguarded by formally recognising the role of village elders as cultural guardians within modern Banaban governance. Integrating their authority into the legal framework of the *Rabi Council of Leaders* would ensure that ancestral knowledge and traditional practices remain central to decision-making.

Village Elder representatives would serve as a vital link between the community and the Council, ensuring that as new governance systems evolve, Banaban heritage is upheld rather than sidelined. By incorporating traditional wisdom into administrative frameworks, Banabans can protect their identity while navigating the complexities of an ever-changing world.

At the same time, the widening *education gap* within Banaban society must be urgently addressed.

Formal education alone will not safeguard Banaban ethnic identity or ensure the survival of their community unless active programs and meaningful development initiatives on Rabi are implemented.

To sustain their future, Banabans must create viable opportunities on Rabi and Banaba for younger generations. Without such prospects, the skills and knowledge gained within the community risk being lost rather than reinvested back into Banaban society.

The Rabi Council of Leaders must spearhead this effort, ensuring a strategic and unified approach to securing Banaban self-sufficiency. A practical solution involves engaging skilled Banabans living and working abroad, enabling them to contribute remotely through:

- Public awareness campaigns
- International advocacy efforts
- Structured participation in sustainable development projects

By taking a leadership role, the Rabi Council of Leaders can bridge the gap between Banaban heritage and modern opportunities, fostering a future where both cultural preservation and economic sustainability thrive.

Additionally, cultural and traditional learning should be formally incorporated into the education curriculum, ensuring younger generations remain deeply connected to their heritage.

24. Banaban MP, Tibanga Taratai (middle back) and Elders residing on Banaba Island 2019 call for independence (Banaban Vision archive).

25. Roabeia Ken Sigrah and Stacey M. King returning Te Aka ancestral remain to Te Aka Clan residing on Rabi Island, 2000. (S.M. King Collection)

24. Honoring Banaban Identity

Above all, Banaban traditions must not be forgotten. While most Banabans today are born on Rabi, their cultural and spiritual identity remains deeply rooted in a homeland many have never seen.

For Banabans, land is both mother and teacher.

Over generations, they have understood that while the land can exist without them, *they cannot exist without the land.*

Their respect for Banaba, shaping their identity and guiding their relationships, must continue to inform how they care for one another and sustain their heritage for future generations.

26. The authors meeting with Dr Lampert at ANU, Canberra 1997 to arrange the return of artefacts recovered from Te Aka dig in 1960s. (S. King Collection 1997).

References

Aiden, C., Ratuvuki, L., Teai, T. *Report of the Committee of Inquiry in to the Rabi Island Council Affairs.* Government Buildings, Suva. Fiji. 8 April 1994.

Bellwood, Peter. *Man's Conquest of the Pacific.* New York, Oxford University Press. 1979 Bingham, Harim. *Gilbertese-English Dictionary.* American Board of Commissioners for Foreign Missions, Boston, USA. 1908

Corrin Care, Jennifer. Conflict between Customary Law and Human Rights in the South Pacific. Presented 12th Commonwealth Law Conference at Kuala Lumpur, September 1999. Core Document Forming Part of the Reports of States Parties; Fiji. United Nations, International Human Rights Instruments. 25 November 1002.

Coming Home to Banaba. Transcript documentary produced by B.B.C. Open University, 1998

Ellice, A.F. *Ocean Island and Nauru.* Sydney: Angus & Robertson Ltd, 1936.

Fraenkel, John. Minority Right in Fiji and The Solomon Island: Reinforcing Constitutional Protections, Establishing Land Rights and Overcoming Poverty. University of the South Pacific. 12-16 May 2003

Grimble, A. From Birth to Death in the Gilbert Islands. Journal of the Royal Anthropological Institute, 1921.

Grimble, A. *Tungaru Traditions*, edited by H.E. Maude. Melbourne University Press, 1989. *Human Rights: A Pacific Agenda.* Closing statement, Amnesty International Australia. 4-5 September 2004.

Grimble, A. *Sketched History of Banaba*, MS in Grimble Papers in the University of Adelaide Archives. n.d.

Irwin, Geoffrey. *Prehistoric Exploration and Colonisation of the Pacific.* Cambridge, Cambridge University Press. 1992

King, Stacey. Interview *Coming Home to Banaba.* Television documentary produced by B.B.C. Open University, 1998

Kiribati Legislation – *The Constitution of Kiribati.* Pacific Law Materials.

Lampert, R.J. *Anthropological Investigation of te Aka Village, Ocean Island: Preliminary Report.* Canberra, Department of Anthropology, Australian National University, 1965.

Lampert, R.J. *An Anthropological Investigation of Ocean Island, Central Pacific.*
Archaeology and Physical Anthropology in Oceania, Vol. 111, No.1. April, 1968

Lennon, Edna. Former wife of BPC employee 1950-1965. Interview conducted by S.King, 1992.

Mahaffy, Arthur. *Ocean Island.* Blackwood's Magazine, November, 1910.

Maude, Harry and Honor. Recorded Interview conducted by K. Sigrah and S. King, Canberra. 1997.

Maude, H.E. *Memorandum on the Future of the Banaban Population of Ocean Island; With Special Relations to their Lands and Funds.* Chief Lands Commissioner, Gilbert and Ellice Islands Colony, 1946.

Maude, H.C. and H.E. *The Book of Banaba.* IPS, University of South Pacific Fiji, 1995. Maude, H.C. and H.E. *The Social Organisation of Banaba or Ocean Island of Banaba or Ocean Island, Central Pacific*, Journal of the Polynesian Society 41, 1932.

Sigrah, Raobeia Ken. Interview, *Coming Home to Banaba.* Television documentary produced by B.B.C. Open University, 1998

Sigrah, Raobeia Ken and King, Stacey M. *Te Rii ni Banaba.* IPS, University of South Pacific Fiji, 2001.

Sivia, Tora. Report on the Pacific Regional Seminar. Director of Culture and Heritage, Ministry of Culture and Heritage, Fiji Island. 11-13 February, 1999.

Walkup, Alfred. *Report of the First Voyage of the Missionary Barkantine 'Morning Star' to Micronesia, 1885.* Boston, American Board of Commissioners for Foreign Missions. 1885 Watson, Lilla. *Welcome: Amnesty International Conference,* Brisbane, 4 Sept 2004 Williams, Maslyn and Macdonald, Barrie. *The Phosphateers.* Melbourne University Press 1985.

About the Authors

RAOBEIA KEN SIGRAH
1956 – 2021

The late Raobeia Ken Sigrah was born on 18 January 1956 on Rabi, Fiji. He identified as a Banaban but held a Fiji passport and later resided in Australia. Known as Ken to his friends, he began his education at the age of seven at Buakonikai Primary School in 1962 and continued at Banaban Primary School until 1967. After passing his Intermediate exams, he attended Niusawa Methodist High School, a Fijian school on nearby Taveuni. In 1980, he studied English for a year at Fulton College in Fiji.

In 1972, Ken was employed as a clerk for the Rabi Council of Leaders in the Public Works Department. Around this time, he joined the Banaban Dancing Group, which represented the Council culturally and performed abroad. That same year, Ken travelled with the group at the invitation of Australian authorities to perform at the opening ceremonies of the Sydney Opera House, facilitated by the Fiji Arts Theatre. The group also performed in Brisbane during the tour. In 1974, Ken toured Nauru, Banaba, and Tarawa with the dancing group while still working as a clerk for the Rabi Council. In 1975, he attended the South Pacific Festival of Arts in Rotorua, New Zealand. After this trip, he left the dancing group but continued working for the Rabi Council.

In 1979, Ken joined a group of young Banaban men and elders on a significant trip to Banaba just before mining operations ceased. After nine months on Banaba, he returned to Rabi. By 1982, he was employed by the Fiji government as a clerk and storeman, a position he held for six years until he resigned in 1989. He was then re-employed by the Rabi Council as a Labour Officer and Inspector. He resigned again from the Council in 1990 and returned to a traditional Banaban lifestyle.

Ken studied Banaban culture and customs under the guidance of Banaban elders. He began these studies at the age of 14, as part of his responsibilities as a male clan member, preparing to serve as a clan spokesman in meetings concerning Banaban culture, customs, and genealogies. Ken witnessed the challenges his people faced and represented individual clans in general meetings, exchanging ideas with Banaban elders. His first experience as a clan spokesman was in 1987, followed by further roles in 1994, 1995, and 1996.

In 1997, Ken asked Stacey King to assist him in writing a history of Banaba. His aim was to promote Banaban history, culture, and customs, though he had previously struggled to find a sponsor for editing and publishing the work. With many elders having passed away and others in their later years, he hoped to publish this material, gathered over many years, for the benefit of the younger Banaban generation, who are now growing up in a different environment, to help them preserve their culture, heritage, and identity as Banabans.

STACEY M. KING

Stacey M. King is a historian, author, entrepreneur, and philanthropist. She has been an advocate for the indigenous Banaban people for many decades.

In 1989, she began researching her family's history for a historical novel based on their lives titled – *Nakaa's Awakening: Land of Matang* (Book One; 2000).

In 1997, she formed a personal and collaborative partnership with the late Ken Raobeia Sigrah, a Banaban Clan historian and spokesperson. Their first published work, *Te Rii Ni Banaba – backbone of Banaba* (2001; 2019), is a history book written from an indigenous perspective and endorsed by Banaban Clan elders.

With the establishment of Banaban Vision Publications, Stacey is converting much of their writings and research findings into digital publications. Since the passing of her beloved partner, Raobeia Ken Sigrah, she has been determined to continue his legacy in preserving Banaban history for future generations.

27. Stacey M. King (left) and Raobeia Ken Sigrah (right) meeting with R.H. Peter McGauran (centre), Australian Multicultural Affairs Minister in Brisbane 2004.

Other Titles By The Authors

Banaban History Non-Fiction Book
Te Rii ni Banaba backbone of Banaba. First Edition: IPS, Suva, Fiji. 2001, Second edition, Banaban Vision Publications, Gold Coast, Australia 2019.
Australia Banaba Relations: the Price of Shaping a Nation. Banaban Vision, Gold Coast, March 2023.
Legacy of a Miner's daughter: the impact on the Banabans after phosphate mining. Banaban Vision Publications, Gold Coast, Australia 2023.
Banaban Cultural Identity. Banaban Vision Australia 2024.

History Non-Fiction Book – Chapter in Book
The Banaba-Ocean Island chronicles: private collections, indigenous record-keeping, fact and fiction. Chapter 17, *Hunting the Collectors.* Cambridge Scholars, UK.

Historical Fiction
Nakaa's Awakening, Land of Matang. Banaban Vision Publications, Gold Coast, Australia, 2020 (Book 1; 4-book series. Blend of history, biography and fictional reconstruction)

Articles and Presentations
Australia Banaba Relations: the price of shaping a nation is now a call for recognition. Adapted from Conference Paper: The Pacific in Australia 2006.
This paper was presented at The Pacific in Australia - Australia in the Pacific conference QUT, Carseldine campus, Brisbane, Australia 24 to 27 January 2006 - The Pacific and Australia - Australia in the Pacific; Humanities research - History.
Banaba-Ocean Island Chronicles: Private collections and indigenous record-keeping proving fact from fiction. Conference Paper: The Pacific in Australia 2006. This paper was presented at The Pacific in Australia - Australia in the Pacific conference QUT, Carseldine campus, Brisbane, Australia 24 to 27 January 2006 - The Pacific and Australia - Australia in the Pacific; Humanities research - History.
Cultural Identity of Banabans
Adapted from a Conference Paper: ISLANDS of the WORLD VIII Taiwan. This paper was presented and published at ISLANDS of the WORLD VIII International Conference "Changing Islands –

Changing Worlds"1-7 November 2004, Kinmen Island (Quemoy), Taiwan.

Legacy of a Miners Daughter and Assessment of the Social Changes of the Banabans after Phosphate Mining on Banaba

Adapted from a Conference Paper: ISLANDS of the WORLD VIII Taiwan. This paper was presented and published at ISLANDS of the WORLD VIII International Conference "Changing Islands – Changing Worlds"1-7 November 2004, Kinmen Island (Quemoy), Taiwan.

Essentially Being Banaban in Today's World: The Role of Banaban Law, Te Rii Ni Banaba (Backbone of Banaba) in a Changing World.

Conference Paper: ISLANDS of the WORLD VIII Taiwan. This paper was presented and published at ISLANDS of the WORLD VIII International Conference "Changing Islands – Changing Worlds"1-7 November 2004, Kinmen Island (Quemoy), Taiwan.

Banaban Social Media sites by Authors
Abara Banaba—Come Meet the Banabans:
banaban.com
Banaban Vision: banabanvision.com
Banaban Voice Facebook:
facebook.com/groups/banabanvoice/

Banaban Vision: banabanvision.com
Banaban Media: vocalmedia.com

Connect:
Banaban Vision Publications
PO Box 1116 Paradise Point Qld 4216 Australia
Stacey M. King – Author's Page: staceymking.com
Email: admin@banaban.com
Raobeia Ken Sigrah – Author's Page:
https://www.banabanvision.com/raobeia-ken-sigrah
Te Rii Ni Banaba -Facebook group:
https://www.facebook.com/groups/296299534653304/
Linkedin: Stacey King:
https://www.linkedin.com/in/stacey-king-4ba68a76/

www.ingramcontent.com/pod-product-compliance
Lightning Source LLC
Chambersburg PA
CBHW071910070526
44583CB00016B/1924